Poems About Cheese

by Stevie Swift

©stevie swift 2023

This book is for everyone who cheers me on while I do weird things like write poems about cheese.

&

This book is for everyone who thinks I'm nuts and should go practice law, or do something else considered a "real" job. I hope this book encourages you to relax a little, to eat more cheese, and to mind your own mouse wax.

Hungry

Why aren't there more
Songs about pizza?
Or more sonnets
Written to cheese?
More art with
Donuts & Cupcakes?
More movies
With pie in the lead?
Seems pretty
Messed up to me
But you know what?
I might just be hungry

Queso

Cheese won't solve all
the world's problems,
I know.

But I imagine a few
might be better
with queso

Healthy People Do

Here is something true:
Healthy people DO
But we aren't all healthy all the time,
so sometimes people don't.
"I'd love to sit around eating cheese all day,"
we say, but we joke!

It might be fun for a day or a week,
then it won't.
Because healthy people want to DO;
unhealthy people don't.
And the solution isn't to
MAKE THEM DO STUFF
It's to heal them with love
while they won't

Abs

Cheese tastes better
than six pack abs feel
I don't know from experience
but I'm sure this is real

It's Mean

It's mean to trap mice
With their favorite thing
It's mean, mean, mean
How would you like it
If you were having a DAY
And looked up to find an overflowing plate
You give it a sniff
A big, juicy whiff
You say to yourself "Right,
I think I just might."
You reach for your snack -
And SNAP! CRUNCH! CRACK!
It's mean
It's mean to trap mice with their favorite thing
It's just mean.

More Relatable Than Notting Hill

I'm just a girl
Standing in front of a fridge
Asking it to feed me

I'm just a girl
Standing in front of a fridge
Asking it to have cheese

Comfort Zones

There is a time for getting
Out of comfort zones
A time for letting
People drag you from home

And there's a time to stay
In your comfortable sheets
Beneath a big, fat tray
Of cheeses and meats

Comfort zones are fine
Sometimes
I sure like mine

Cheese Advertisement?

Among the world's
most useless things,
I'm sure, are
advertisements for cheese

Healing

Cheese will not heal the world's wounds
But I'm convinced
It's the people
Who know how to stop and enjoy the things they love –
Like cheese, and books, and pecan pie –
Who know how to stop and enjoy the people they love –
Who know themselves
I'm convinced it is they who will heal
And who will show us how to heal too

Name That Tune

The following poems are parodies
of popular songs and I've made each
of them better by adding cheese

try this at home, with broccoli

I Hope You Don't Mind

I hope you don't mind
I hope you don't mind
I won't put down these curds
How wonderful life is
With cheese in the world

Take Me To Cheese

Take me to cheese
I'll worship like a rat
At the shrine of your rind
I'll tell you my order
You can sharpen your knife
Offer me that perfect wedge
O' cheese, let me get a bit more
Take me to cheese

Poems About Cheese.

Sweet Parmesan

Where it began, with lactic acid bacteria
And then it's curdled nice and strong
Was in a wheel
Stored through a couple summers
Who'd have believed you'd come along
Sweet parmesan
Ba Ba Ba
Pasta never seemed so good
I drown all mine
In a pound just like we should

so good so good so good

I Love You Baked Brie

I love you baked brie
And if it's quite alright
I need you baked brie
To warm the lonely nights
I love you baked brie
Trust in my when I say

Oh pretty baked brie
I'm gonna clean that plate
Oh let me love you baked brie
Let me love you

If You Like It Then You Better Put Some Cheese On It

If you like pizza you
better put some cheese on it

If you like nachos you
better put some cheese on 'em

If you like pretzels
you better put some cheese on 'em

oh oh oh, oh oh oh oh

CHEEEEEEEEESE!

Fly Me To The Moon

Fly me to the moon
Let me eat the cheese up there
I don't care how far it is
This gouda is my air

In other words
I love cheese
In other words
Slice some cheddar please

Give Me Your Answer, Do

Cream cheese
Cream cheese
Jarlsburg and gouda too
I'm half crazy all for the love of you

There won't be a stylish platter
I'll eat you so fast it won't matter

And you'll look sweet
Between my teeth
On this cracker I got just for you

Resolution

Take more naps
Eat more cheese

Do you need a mid-year resolution?
Feel free to borrow these

A Conversation

Me:
I'll whine for cheese
Cry for cheese
Stand in line for cheese
Commit crimes for cheese
Lie for cheese

Cashier:

blinks

Me:

J/K, but I'd very much like to buy some cheese

Schedule

The best kind of schedule is
The kind of schedule
With nothing much on schedule at all
Then any old afternoon
When I have nothing much to do
I can spend time with crackers and a cheese ball

Be Kind

Being kind
doesn't mean
someone likes what you say
Being kind means
it needed said and
you found a compassionate way
a way with the gentleness you'd
hope to be treated with
and a way with a cheese basket
if a situation needed it.

Do Weird Things

Do weird things that make you happy
like ordering dessert first
Don't let boring people make you feel crappy
For following a harmless urge

Text someone they're awesome
Buy yourself a half-birthday cake
Write a poem about a cheese-eating possum
Whatever improves your day

Do weird things that make you happy
Dont let boring people make you feel crappy

Love Of Money

I love
money
I can do a
neat trick
where I turn it
into
cheese

For Every Occasion

For every occasion,
bring peace

Whoever gathered,
however many, whatever for —

you know you can
be the one

Who brings peace

And if you can't
Then at the very least

Bring cheese

The Cheese Poet & The Sloth

The cheese poet and the sloth
They are the same
Neither are trying
To win someone's race
Both choose to move
At their own perfect pace
You might call them lazy
As you pass on your way
They can't hear you over
The sound of a peaceful day

This is Love

Leave me
One cube, one
Very large cube of
Enchanting, extraordinary cheese

Love of Cheese

Love of cheese
will solve a
multitude of problems

Poems About Cheese.

Love You More

I love you more than cheese
and that's saying a lot
'cause cheese has always been there
when people have not

cheese, thick and melted
between soft slices of bread
and cheese dipped in soup
then shoved in my head

but you're pretty cool for a person
I kinda like the way you sneeze
and I like other stuff too, so yeah -
you're better than cheese

I Wear a Lot of Hats (Literally)

It's rare to see me without a hat
People say, "You have hair!"
"I had no idea what was under there!"

They ask, "What's with the hats?"
And maybe they expect a story
I'm afraid to say, though, my answer is boring

It doesn't hurt anyone
And it makes me happy

It's the same reason I do a lot of things
Like writing poems about cheese

It doesn't hurt anyone
And it makes me happy

Once Upon A Time

Once upon a time, there was a princess in a tower
She was trapped, and stranded, and starving
more by the hour
"Hello!" She cried out to no one but trees
Her voice floated away on the cool autumn breeze
It floated and floated and floated some more
It drifted over mountains and past a purple sea shore

It floated until it found a sympathetic ear
On the head of a fairy named Wibbledy Shear
And Wibbledy flew just as fast as he could
To the stranded princess in the deserted wood
He perched on the window with a gentle swish
To offer the Princess a single wish

Ask me for anything - anything you please
Without pausing, the princess said,
"A Lifetime of Cheese"
Wibbledy gasped! "Don't you want to be free?"
"No, thanks," said the princess, I'm happy just me
"Thank you so much for coming!
Now, where is that cheese?"

Will There Be Cheese?

Oh but,
Will there be cheese?

Because,
I have cheese
here at home

The World Is Hard

The world is
hard, but
cheese is good

Cheese is how it should
be
Cheese is simple,
is delightful

The world is
hard but
cheese is good

Eat some cheese
enjoy something simple
be delighted

Chizu Haikus

These chizu haikus
in honor of hokkaido
the cheese capital

Cheese & My Pants

Cheese is delicious
My pants don't fit anymore
Cheese is delicious

Poems About Cheese.

Twitter

Twitter is garbage
Red-faced, loud, screeching garbage
Just eat cheese instead

X

X is still garbage
Red-faced, loud, screeching garbage
Just eat cheese instead

Nightmare

I dreamt of a world
devoid, bereft, free of cheese
I had a nightmare

Look Away

Please don't look at me
As I eat all of the cheese
Let me be alone

Cheese vs Chips

Someone asked if I'd rather
have cheese or chips
Well listen here,
I'm snacking on my favorite pick
A family-sized bag of
sour cream and cheddar crisps

This thing, sir, that you've asked of me
Is an ugly, hateful, false dichotomy

Both/and is a thing, sir
Both/and is a thing.

But First A Cheese Snack

Feeling overwhelmed by the cracks in this world?
By the suffering?
By the injustice?
I know it seems like you need to do something,
Like you need to fix everything
But I submit to you
Maybe
Since you can't fix everything
Maybe you could take that overwhelmed feeling
and go somewhere safe

Maybe you could eat some cheese in your pajamas
Maybe you could take some deep breaths
Maybe you could get a hug
And then maybe, when you're
not overwhelmed by everything,
you'll be able to do something.
Not a one of us can fix everything,
but everyone can do something
Sometimes we just need a cheese snack first is all

Sleep

Sleep is not lazy
That's banana crap crazy
I'm certain you don't get enough
So now you're making some up!
And besides, it's not hurting me any
How much or when you sleep
It's not affecting me a single iota
I'm just busy over here eating cheese

So get some sleep!
Good grief, and leave the shame
If anyone is calling you lazy -
Send me their names
I'll send them cheese fast
Because they need to relax

Single Word Poetry

I don't know if you've heard
But you can write a poem
With a single word
You can find one
So precious and beautiful
You say it and - done

You can say
This one word
And know you've conveyed

Everything
With a single thing
Just one beautiful thing
Let it ring

I'll start
And I think
You know
What it it will be -

Cheese.

Let's Go To The Moon

If the moon is made of cheese,
I say, "Let's all go!"
Let's build a swiss cheese boat
To sail a lake of asiago.
Let's live in a house of cheddar
And sit in a gouda chair
Let's kick back at the grilled cheese bar
And eat together under the stars

Ask This Instead

Instead of
"What'd you do this weekend?"
Instead of
"Where'd you go?"
I wonder if there's a better question,
One to encourage slow

Could we ask -

"Did you rest?"
"Did you get some great sleep?"
"Did you take a walk?"
"Did you eat some good cheese?"

Did you take deep breaths while staring into the night sky?
Did you read your favorite book with snacks in bed?
wonder if we can skip "What'd you do and where'd you go?"
And ask about naps and snacks instead.

Try Again With Snacks

Can I just - just be
Here in this place of peace
Everything calm, quiet, clear
Don't make me leave
Don't drag me screaming back
And if you must return to speak to me
Return with snacks

Acapella

Did you know Acapella
Is a type of cheese
AND a way to sing as well?

Let's sing a song
About Acapella
The cheese will be instrumental.

Inviting Your Introvert

I'm bored, will you come over please?
-No.

I'll put out a platter of cheese.
-Maybe.

You don't have to talk to me.
-Okay.

Content

Do I have a place to sit and read?
Do I have some money to buy my cheese?
Do I have a roof to keep me dry?
Do I have a fire to sit beside?
Do I have some friends who sit with me?
Do I have a pot for coffee and tea?
Do I have a project or two or three?
Are they a small gift to the world from me?
Well, then, I don't think I need one more cent
To sit under this roof, to call me content

Adorable

Sometimes you don't want cheese
Instead, you want something sweet
Obviously this doesn't mean
Cheese is suddenly deplorable

People are like this too
It's almost never about you
Try to remember this truth
You're definitely adorable

Life Found

In my teens I couldn't wait
To get out of this world
I was a sad, lonely, angry girl

In my twenties I wanted
To go out in a blaze of glory
I couldn't fathom making it to 40

But I'm here
I made it somehow
You know what I want now?

I want to get old
I want great books to read
I want platters piled with fruit and cheese

I want great conversations
With fascinating faces
And I want to see so many more places

I want to litter my life
With creativity, generosity, kindness
I'm so glad that sad, lonely girl lived to find this

Revenge

Revenge is best served cold
Cheese is best served old
But I don't care how sweet
Revenge might be
I'd rather have cheese
It's like gold

Green Eggs & Ham & Cheese

There's a thing he didn't ask - that Sam I Am
He didn't ask if Guy liked green eggs and ham
With cheese
I mean, please
That's a deal Guy would have took
But it would have been a much shorter book

Bring Cheese

I don't feel well
So you want to bring soup

And that's nice -
It's a sweet thing to do

It's just -I don't
Want the chicken broth kind
I want broccoli & cheddar
Flavored with parmesan rinds

I want potato and cheese
Or some other cheesy stew

Actually, I think I want cheese
Not soup

Lay It On Thick

Cheese is to dinner like joy is to life
On a bad day, lay that joy on thick

Know those thing that bring you joy
And treat it like cheese on broccoli

Problem Solver

Food is not the solution
To my problems
I know

If I stopped to dip
Some food in cheese
It wouldn't hurt though

A Life I Can Stand

I'd rather live a life others
Don't understand
Than a life
I can't stand.

They don't have to know
What the cheese poets know
About how beautiful & hard
It is to go slow

They don't have to know
They don't have to understand
It's up to me
To live a life I can stand

Hero

Captain America is great, like really really great
But sometimes I want a hero to show up
with a cheesy plate and say
"It's late - take this plate to the bath
And here's a diet coke, go on relax
Don't worry I'm not staying -
I'm off to do more day saving."

Always

Roses are red, sometimes
Violets are blue, most times
Grass is green (when healthy and in season)
Cheese is delicious, always.

10 Things I Hate About Cheese

I hate the way you're always there
And the way you come in slices
I hate how you're the perfect car snack
And I hate when you come with spices

I hate your big dumb deliciousness
I hate that you're perfectly divine
I hate you so much it makes me hungry
And even makes me rhyme

I hate the way you taste so good
And then attack my insides
I hate it when you're delightfully creamy
Spread on crackers - I could cry

I hate it when you're not in the house
When I've searched it wall to wall
But mostly I hate that way I don't hate you
Not even close, not even a little, not even at all

Accio Cheese

When life plain sucks
And it's all down the tube
Accio cheese

When the decisions pile up
But you don't have a clue
Accio cheese

When the days are too full
And you need less to do
Accio cheese

It won't solve your life
But when you need a moment just you
Accio cheese

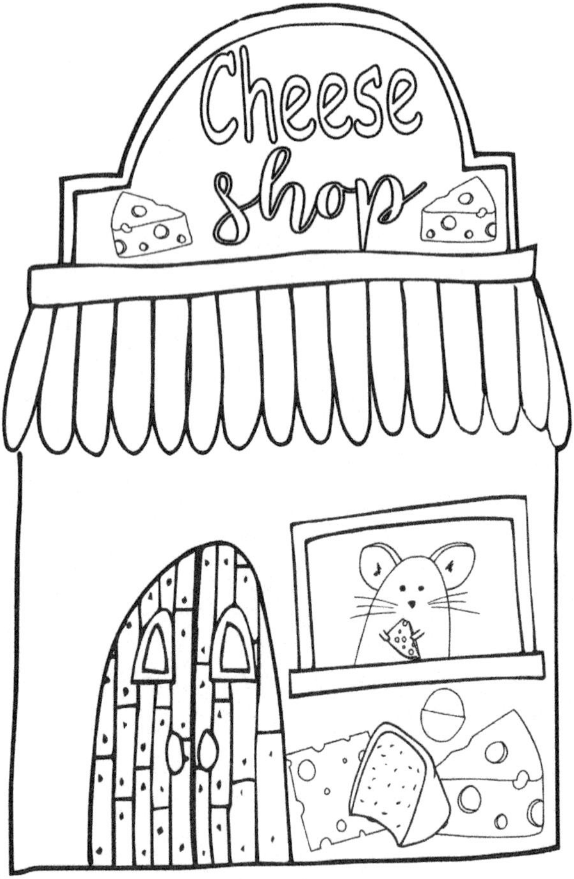
Cheese
shop

The Happiest Story

Once upon a time
I had some cheese
And we lived happily ever after

THE END

Poems About Cheese.

Printed in Great Britain
by Amazon